Beardsley's Illustrations for

LE MORTE DARTHUR

Reproduced in Facsimile
from the Dent Edition of 1893-94

Arranged by
EDMUND V. GILLON, Jr.

Dover Publications, Inc., New York

Published in Canada by General Publishing Company, Ltd., 30 Lesmill Road,
Don Mills, Toronto, Ontario.
Published in the United Kingdom by Constable and Company, Ltd.

Beardsley's Illustrations for Le Morte Darthur, first published by Dover
Publications in 1972, includes the complete art and selected pages of text of
Sir Thomas Malory, *Le Morte Darthur,* originally published by J. M. Dent & Co.,
in London, in 1893-1894. A Publisher's Note has been written especially for the
Dover edition.

DOVER *Pictorial Archive* SERIES

International Standard Book Number: 0-486-22348-5
Library of Congress Catalog Card Number: 71-166432

Manufactured in the United States of America
Dover Publications, Inc.
180 Varick Street
New York, N. Y. 10014

PUBLISHER'S NOTE

In 1892 an obscure London publisher named J.M. Dent decided to produce a mammoth work: a fine, illustrated edition of Sir Thomas Malory's *Le Morte Darthur*. Dent was hoping to recoup the losses of a bindery fire, and may have wanted also to rival William Morris and his hand-operated Kelmscott Press — to show that a fine edition could be produced with the then modern line-block and linotype machine.

To illustrate the work he selected, surprisingly, a young insurance-office clerk a few of whose drawings had been shown him by the bookseller Frederick J. Evans. Aubrey Beardsley was then a twenty-year-old art student who spent his lunchhours browsing in Evans' bookshop and seemed endlessly productive in the satiric drawings he turned out at night. A consumptive, Beardsley looked as if he could barely last the winter (and indeed he had only five years for his unparalleled development and influence). His work had been published only in school magazines.

Nevertheless, on the basis of some sketches and a frontispiece ("The Achieving of the Sangreal," p. 70), Dent commissioned Beardsley to illustrate the *Morte Darthur* "in the manner of Burne-Jones" for the sum of 250 pounds. Beardsley thought it would require about 400 black-and-white drawings; the book was to be issued in monthly parts, and the first part was to appear one year from that date.

The first issue appeared eighteen rather than twelve months later, and Beardsley worked a full year beyond that as his projected 400 drawings grew to nearly 585 chapter openings, borders, initials, ornaments and other drawings (all reproduced in this volume), including 20 full- or double-page illustrations. When one considers that Beardsley was already ill and also responsible during this period for his *Salomé* and the editorship of *The Yellow Book,* his productivity on the *Morte Darthur* seems all the more astonishing. This was undoubtedly Beardsley's greatest period: he entered it unknown, and ended it one of the best-known figures in London.

Beardsley might have seemed an unusual choice to illustrate Malory—he was a modern satirist where apparently Dent wanted a thoroughgoing medievalist. While Beardsley had met Burne-Jones and was able to imitate his style, he was much more interested in the new Japanese influence that seemed in conflict with it. The result is a Malory such as the world had never seen, with fauns and satyrs peering from behind the trees, and greater nudity and sexual frankness than one associates with the Middle Ages.

Dent went on to become famous as the publisher of *Everyman's Library;* Beardsley was to die five years later, in 1898, at the age of twenty-five. Dent, hearing the artist was near death, wrote him a touching letter urging him to get well so that he could illustrate—in what would have been a new Beardsley period—*The Pilgrim's Progress.*

Le Morte Darthur originally appeared in twelve parts between June, 1893, and mid-1894, and instructions were given for binding it in two or three volumes (two frontispieces were supplied).

Three hundred copies were printed on Dutch hand-made paper (at 6 *s.* 6 *d.* for each of the twelve parts), and 1500 on smooth gray-green paper (at 2 *s.* 2 *d.* per part). Thus for four or one and a half pounds, with a small sum for binding, one could purchase a book that would cost collectors hundreds of dollars today.

Le Morte Darthur had only modest success, and Dent still had copies in print years later. As time passed, the true significance of the work became clear: it is not only important in the history of bookmaking, as a superb example of the illustrated book, but it is also the work that launched the "Beardsley look" which was to change the appearance of the *fin de siècle* and influence succeeding generations including our own.

The present volume shows all Beardsley's illustrations in their original printed size. Arrangement is by book, in the sequence of the original work.

The Dent edition of Malory is not a particularly accurate one, and is rather difficult to read. Better texts are easily available to the reader today. For that reason, only Beardsley's work has been reproduced here. However, fifteen pages of Book I and the opening page of Books II-XXI have been printed in facsimile, to show how Beardsley's drawings ornament the page.

THE EDITORS

New York, 1972

CONTENTS

Cover design for "Le Morte Darthur" (issued in parts)

Morte Darthur.

How King Arthur saw the Questing Beast, and thereof had great maruel.

THE BIRTH LIFE AND ACTS OF KING ARTHUR OF HIS
NOBLE KNIGHTS OF THE ROUND TABLE THEIR
MARVELLOUS ENQUESTS AND ADVENTURES
THE ACHIEVING OF THE SAN GREAL
AND IN THE END LE MORTE DAR⸗
THUR WITH THE DOLOUROUS
DEATH AND DEPARTING
OUT OF THIS WORLD
OF THEM ALL.

THE TEXT AS WRIT⸗
TEN BY SIR THOMAS MALORY
AND IMPRINTED BY WILLIAM CAXTON
AT WESTMINSTER THE YEAR MCCCCLXXXV AND
NOW SPELLED IN MODERN STYLE.   WITH AN INTRO⸗
DUCTION BY PROFESSOR RHYS AND EMBELLISHED WITH
MANY ORIGINAL DESIGNS BY AUBREY BEARDSLEY.   MDCCCXCIII.

Title page for Volume I

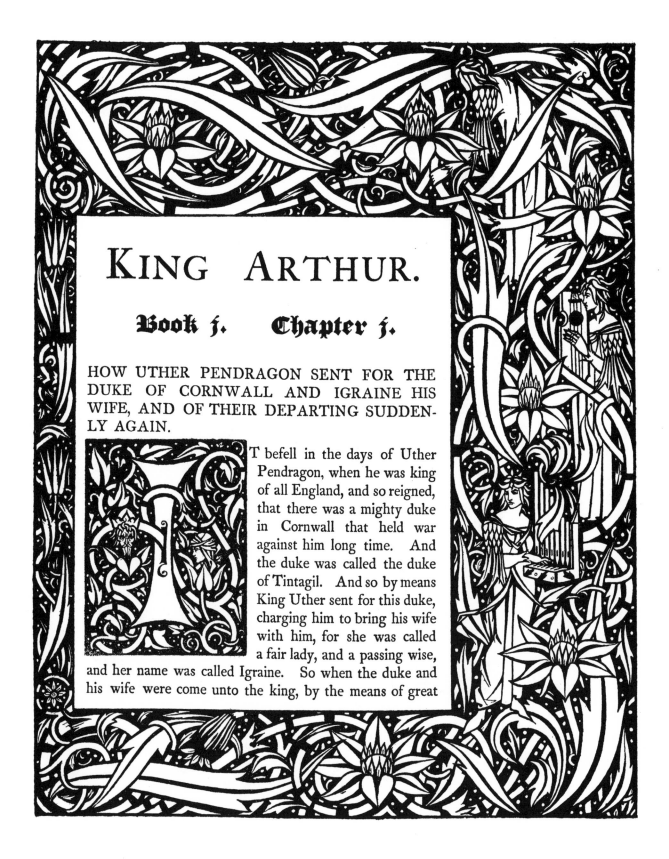

KING ARTHUR.

Book j.   Chapter j.

HOW UTHER PENDRAGON SENT FOR THE DUKE OF CORNWALL AND IGRAINE HIS WIFE, AND OF THEIR DEPARTING SUDDENLY AGAIN.

T befell in the days of Uther Pendragon, when he was king of all England, and so reigned, that there was a mighty duke in Cornwall that held war against him long time. And the duke was called the duke of Tintagil. And so by means King Uther sent for this duke, charging him to bring his wife with him, for she was called a fair lady, and a passing wise, and her name was called Igraine. So when the duke and his wife were come unto the king, by the means of great lords they were accorded both: the king liked and loved this lady well, and he made them great cheer out of measure, and desired to have lain by her. But she was a passing good woman, and would not assent unto the king. And then she told the duke her husband, and said, I suppose that we were sent for that I should be dishonoured, wherefore, husband, I counsel you, that we depart from hence suddenly, that we may ride all night unto our own castle. And in like wise as she said so they departed, that neither the king nor none of his council were ware of their departing. All so soon as King Uther knew of their departing so suddenly, he was wonderly wroth. Then he called to him his privy council, and told them of the sudden departing of the duke and his wife. Then they asked the king to send for the duke and his wife by a great charge; And if he will not come at your summons, then may ye do your best, then have ye cause to make mighty war upon him. So that was done, and the messengers had their answers, and that was this shortly, that neither he nor his wife would not come at him. Then was the king wonderly wroth. And then the king sent him plain word again, and bad him be ready and stuff him and garnish him, for within forty days he would fetch him out of the biggest castle that he had. When the duke had this warning, anon he went and furnished and garnished two strong castles of his, of the which the one hight Tintagil, and the other castle hight Terrabil. So his wife Dame Igraine he put in the castle of Tintagil, and himself he put in the castle of Terrabil, the which had many issues and posterns out. Then in all haste came Uther with a great host, and laid a siege about the castle of Terrabil. And there he pyght many pavilions, and there was great war made on both parties, and much people slain. Then for pure anger and for great love of fair Igraine the king Uther fell sick. So came to the king Uther, Sir Ulfius a noble knight,

accorded = cordially [received].   hight = was called.

pyght = pitched.

and asked the king why he was sick. I shall tell thee, said the king, I am sick for anger and for love of fair Igraine that I may not be hool. Well, my lord, said Sir Ulfius, I shall seek Merlin, and he shall do you remedy, that your heart shall be pleased. So Ulfius departed, and by adventure he met Merlin in a beggar's array, and then Merlin asked Ulfius whom he sought. And he said he had little ado to tell him. Well, said Merlin, I know whom thou seekest, for thou seekest Merlin; therefore seek no farther, for I am he, and if King Uther will well reward me, and be sworn unto me to fulfil my desire, that shall be his honour and profit more than mine, for I shall cause him to have all his desire. All this will I undertake, said Ulfius, that there shall be nothing reasonable but thou shalt have thy desire. Well, said Merlin, he shall have his entente and desire. And therefore, said Merlin, ride on your way, for I will not be long behind.

Chapter ij.

HOW UTHER PENDRAGON MADE WAR ON THE DUKE OF CORNWALL, AND HOW BY THE MEANS OF MERLIN HE LAY BY THE DUCHESS & GAT ARTHUR. Then Ulfius was glad, and rode on more than a paas till that he came to king Uther Pendragon, and told him he had met with Merlin. Where is he? said the king. Sir, said Ulfius, he will not dwell long; therewithal Ulfius was ware where Merlin stood at the porch of the pavilion's door. And then Merlin was bound to come to the king. When King Uther saw him, he said he was welcome. Sir, said Merlin, I know all your heart every deal; so ye will be sworn unto me as ye be a true king anointed, to

hool = healed.　　　　entente = purpose.
more than a paas = at a very great pace.

fulfil my desire, ye shall have your desire. Then the king was sworn upon the four Evangelists. Sir, said Merlin, this is my desire: the first night that ye shall lie by Igraine ye shall get a child on her, and when that is born, that it shall be delivered to me for to nourish there as I will have it; for it shall be your worship, and the child's avail as mickle as the child is worth. I will well, said the king, as thou wilt have it. Now make you ready, said Merlin, this night ye shall lie with Igraine in the castle of Tintagil, and ye shall be like the duke her husband, Ulfius shall be like Sir Brastias, a knight of the dukes, and I will be like a knight that hight Sir Jordans, a knight of the dukes. But wayte ye make not many questions with her nor her men, but say ye are diseased, and so hie you to bed, and rise not on the morn till I come to you, for the castle of Tintagil is but ten miles hence; so this was done as they devised. But the duke of Tintagil espied how the king rode from the siege of Terrabil, and therefore that night he issued out of the castle at a postern for to have distressed the king's host. And so, through his own issue, the duke himself was slain or ever the king came at the castle of Tintagil. So after the death of the duke, King Uther lay with Igraine more than three hours after his death, and begat on her that night Arthur, and or day came Merlin came to the king, and bade him make him ready, and so he kissed the lady Igraine and departed in all haste. But when the lady heard tell of the duke her husband, and by all record he was dead or ever King Uther came to her; then she marvelled who that might be that lay with her in likeness of her lord; so she mourned privily and held her peace. Then all the barons by one assent prayed the king of accord betwixt the lady Igraine and him; the king gave them leave, for fain would he have been accorded with her. So the king put all the trust in Ulfius to entreat between them, so by the entreaty at the last the king and she met together. Now will we do well, said Ulfius, our king is a lusty

wayte = watch.   diseased = tired.   accord = agreement.

knight and wifeless, and my lady Igraine is a passing fair lady; it were great joy unto us all, an it might please the king to make her his queen. Unto that they all well accorded and moved it to the king. And anon, like a lusty knight, he assented thereto with good will, and so in all haste they were married in a morning with great mirth and joy. And King Lot of Lothian and of Orkney then wedded Margawse that was Gawaine's mother, and King Nentres of the land of Garlot wedded Elaine. All this was done at the request of King Uther. And the third sister Morgan le Fay was put to school in a nunnery, and there she learned so much that she was a great clerk of necromancy, and after she was wedded to King Uriens of the land of Gore that was Sir Ewain's le Blanchemains father.

Chap. iij.

OF THE BIRTH OF KING ARTHUR AND OF HIS NURTURE. Ꭷ Then Queen Igraine waxed daily greater and greater, so it befell after within half a year, as King Uther lay by his queen, he asked her, by the faith she owed to him, whose was the child within her body; then was she sore abashed to give answer. Dismay you not, said the king, but tell me the truth, and I shall love you the better, by the faith of my body. Sir, said she, I shall tell you the truth. The same night that my lord was dead, the hour of his death, as his knights record, there came into my castle of Tintagil a man like my lord in speech and in countenance, and two knights with him in likeness of his two knights Brastias and Jordans, and so I went unto bed with him as I ought to do with my lord, and the same night, as I shall answer unto God, this child was begotten upon me. That is truth, said the king, as ye say; for it was I myself that came in the likeness, and therefore dismay you not, for I am father of the child;

and there he told her all the cause, how it was by Merlin's counsel. Then the queen made great joy when she knew who was the father of her child. Soon came Merlin unto the king, and said, Sir, ye must purvey you for the nourishing of your child. As thou wilt, said the king, be it. Well, said Merlin, I know a lord of yours in this land, that is a passing true man and a faithful, and he shall have the nourishing of your child, and his name is Sir Ector, and he is a lord of fair livelihood in many parts in England and Wales; and this lord, Sir Ector, let him be sent for, for to come and speak with you, and desire him yourself, as he loveth you, that he will put his own child to nourishing to another woman, and that his wife nourish yours. And when the child is born let it be delivered to me at yonder privy postern unchristened. So like as Merlin devised it was done. And when Sir Ector was come he made fyaunce to the king for to nourish the child like as the king desired; and there the king granted Sir Ector great rewards. Then when the lady was delivered, the king commanded two knights and two ladies to take the child, bound in a cloth of gold, and that ye deliver him to what poor man ye meet at the postern gate of the castle. So the child was delivered unto Merlin, and so he bare it forth unto Sir Ector, and made an holy man to christen him, and named him Arthur; and so Sir Ector's wife nourished him with her own pappe.

OF THE DEATH OF KING UTHER PENDRAGON. Then within two years King Uther fell sick of a great malady. And in the meanwhile his enemies usurped upon him, and did a great battle upon his men, and slew many of his people. Sir, said Merlin, ye may not lie so as ye do, for ye must to the field though ye ride on an horse litter: for ye shall never have the better of your enemies but if your person be there, and then shall ye have the victory. So it

purvey = provide.   fyaunce = promise.

MERLIN TAKETH THE
CHILD ARTHVR INTO
HIS KEEPING

was done as Merlin had devised, and they carried the king forth in an horse litter with a great host towards his enemies. And at St. Albans there met with the king a great host of the North. And that day Sir Ulfius and Sir Brastias did great deeds of arms, and King Uther's men overcame the Northern battle and slew many people, and put the remnant to flight. And then the king returned unto London, and made great joy of his victory. And then he fell passing sore sick, so that three days and three nights he was speechless: wherefore all the barons made great sorrow, and asked Merlin what counsel were best. There is none other remedy, said Merlin, but God will have his will. But look ye, all barons, be before King Uther to-morn, and God and I shall make him to speak. So on the morn all the barons with Merlin came before the king; then Merlin said aloud unto King Uther, Sir, shall your son Arthur be king after your days, of this realm with all the appurtenance? Then Uther Pendragon turned him, and said in hearing of them all, I give him God's blessing and mine, and bid him pray for my soul, and righteously and worshipfully that he claim the crown upon forfeiture of my blessing, and therewith he yielded up the ghost, and then was he interred as longed to a king. Wherefore the queen, fair Igraine, made great sorrow, and all the barons.

HOW ARTHUR WAS CHOSEN KING, AND OF WONDERS AND MARVELS OF A SWORD TAKEN OUT OF A STONE BY THE SAID ARTHUR. ❧ Then stood the realm in great jeopardy long while, for every lord that was mighty of men made him strong, and many weened to have been king. Then Merlin went to the Archbishop of Canterbury, and counselled him for to send for all the lords of the realm, and all the gentlemen of arms, that they should to London come by Christmas, upon pain of cursing; and for this cause, that Jesus, that was born on that night, that he would of his great mercy show some miracle, as he was come to be king of mankind, for to show some miracle who should be rightways king of this realm. So the Archbishop, by the advice of Merlin, sent for all the lords and gentlemen of arms that they should come by Christmas even unto London. And many of them made them clean of their life, that their prayer might be the more acceptable unto God. So in the greatest church of London, whether it were Paul's or not the French book maketh no mention, all the estates were long or day in the church for to pray. And when matins and the first mass was done, there was seen in the churchyard, against the high altar, a great stone four square, like unto a marble stone, and in midst thereof was like an anvil of steel a foot on high, and therein stuck a fair sword naked by the point, and letters there were written in gold about the sword that said thus:—Whoso pulleth out this sword of this stone and anvil, is rightwise king born of all England. Then the people marvelled, and told it to the Archbishop. I command, said the Archbishop, that ye keep you within your church, and pray unto God still; that no man touch the sword till the high mass be all done. So when all masses were done all the lords went to behold the stone and the sword. And when they saw the scripture, some essayed; such as would have been king. But none might stir the sword nor move it. He is not here, said the Archbishop, that shall achieve the sword, but doubt not God will make him known. But this is my counsel, said the Archbishop, that we let purvey ten knights, men of good fame, and they to keep this sword. So it was ordained, and then there was made a cry, that every man should essay that would, for to win the sword. And upon New Year's Day the barons let make a jousts and a tournament, that all knights that would joust or tourney there might play, and all this was ordained for to keep the lords and the commons together, for the Archbishop trusted that God would make him known that should win the sword. So upon New Year's Day, when the service was done, the barons rode unto the field, some to joust and some to tourney, and so it happened that Sir Ector, that had great livelihood about London, rode unto the jousts, and with him rode Sir Kay his son, and young Arthur that was his nourished brother; and Sir Kay was made knight at All Hallow mass afore. So as they rode to the jousts-ward, Sir Kay had lost his sword, for he had left it at his father's lodging, and so he prayed young Arthur for to ride for his sword. I will well, said Arthur, and rode fast after the sword, and when he came home, the lady and all were out to see the jousting. Then was Arthur wroth, and said to himself, I will ride to the churchyard, and take the sword with me that sticketh in the stone, for my brother Sir Kay shall not be without a sword this day. So when he came to the churchyard, Sir Arthur alit and tied his horse to the stile, and so he went to the tent, and found no knights there, for they were at jousting; and so he handled the sword by the handles, and lightly and fiercely pulled it out of the stone, and took his horse and rode his way until he came to his brother Sir Kay, and delivered him the sword. And as soon as Sir Kay saw the sword, he wist well it was the sword of the stone, and so he rode to his father Sir Ector, and said: Sir, lo here is the sword of the stone, wherefore I must be king of this land. When Sir Ector beheld the sword, he returned again and came to the church, and there they alit all three, and went into the church. And anon he made Sir Kay to swear upon a book how he came to that sword. Sir, said Sir Kay, by my brother Arthur, for he brought it to me. How gat ye this sword? said Sir Ector to Arthur. Sir, I will tell you. When I came home for my brother's sword, I found nobody at home to deliver me his sword, and so I thought my brother Sir Kay should not be swordless, and so I came hither eagerly and pulled it out of the stone without any pain. Found ye any knights about this sword, said Sir Ector. Nay, said Arthur. Now, said Sir Ector to Arthur, I understand ye must be king of this land. Wherefore I, said Arthur, and for what cause? Sir, said Ector, for God will have it so, for there should never man have drawn out this sword, but he that shall be rightways king of this land. Now let me see whether ye can put the sword there as it was, and pull it out again. That is no mastery, said Arthur, and so he put it in the stone, therewithal Sir Ector essayed to pull out the sword and failed.

HOW KING ARTHUR PULLED OUT THE SWORD DIVERS TIMES. Now essay, said Sir Ector unto Sir Kay. And anon he pulled at the sword with all his might, but it would not be. Now shall ye essay, said Sir Ector to Arthur. I will well, said Arthur, and pulled it out easily. And therewithal Sir Ector knelt down to the earth, and Sir Kay. Alas, said Arthur, my own dear father and brother, why kneel ye to me? Nay, nay, my lord Arthur, it is not so, I was never your father nor of your blood, but I wot well ye are of an higher blood than I weened ye were. And then Sir Ector told him all, how he was bitaken him for to nourish him, and by whose commandment, and by Merlin's deliverance. Then Arthur made great doole when he understood that Sir Ector was not his father. Sir, said Ector unto Arthur, will ye be my good and gracious lord when ye are king. Else were I to blame, said Arthur, for ye are the man in the world

bitaken = entrusted.   doole = grief.

that I am most beholden to, and my good lady and mother your wife, that as well as her own hath fostered me and kept. And if ever it be God's will that I be king as ye say, ye shall desire of me what I may do, and I shall not fail you, God forbid I should fail you. Sir, said Sir Ector, I will ask no more of you, but that ye will make my son, your foster brother, Sir Kay, seneschal of all your lands. That shall be done, said Arthur, and more, by the faith of my body, that never man shall have that office but he, while he and I live. Therewithal they went unto the Archbishop, and told him how the sword was achieved, and by whom; and on Twelfth-day all the barons came thither, and to essay to take the sword, who that would essay. But there afore them all, there might none take it out but Arthur; wherefore there were many lords wroth, and said it was great shame unto them all and the realm, to be over-governed with a boy of no high blood born, and so they fell out at that time that it was put off till Candlemas, and then all the barons should meet there again; but always the ten knights were ordained to watch the sword day and night, and so they set a pavilion over the stone and the sword, and five always watched. So at Candlemas many more great lords came thither for to have won the sword, but there might none prevail. And right as Arthur did at Christmas, he did at Candlemas, and pulled out the sword easily, whereof the barons were sore agrieved and put it off in delay till the high feast of Easter. And as Arthur sped before, so did he at Easter, yet there were some of the great lords had indignation that Arthur should be king, and put it off in a delay till the feast of Pentecost. Then the Archbishop of Canterbury by Merlyn's providence let purvey then of the best knights that they might get, and such knights as Uther Pendragon loved best and most trusted in his days. And such knights were put about Arthur as Sir Baudwin of Britain, Sir Kay, Sir Ulfius, Sir Brastias. All these with many other, were always about Arthur, day and night, till the feast of Pentecost.

HOW KING ARTHUR WAS CROWNED, AND HOW HE MADE OFFICERS. And at the feast of Pentecost all manner of men essayed to pull at the sword that would essay, but none might prevail but Arthur, and pulled it out afore all the lords and commons that were there, wherefore all the commons cried at once, We will have Arthur unto our king, we will put him no more in delay, for we all see that it is God's will that he shall be our king, and who that holdeth against it, we will slay him. And therewith they all kneeled at once, both rich and poor, and cried Arthur mercy because they had delayed him so long, and Arthur forgave them, and took the sword between both his hands, and offered it upon the altar where the Archbishop was, and so was he made knight of the best man that was there. And so anon was the coronation made. And there was he sworn unto his lords and the commons for to be a true king, to stand with true justice from thenceforth the days of this life. Also then he made all lords that held of the crown to come in, and to do service as they ought to do. And many complaints were made unto Sir Arthur of great wrongs that were done since the death of King Uther, of many lands that were bereaved lords, knights, ladies, and gentlemen. Wherefore King Arthur made the lands to be given again unto them that owned them. When this was done, that the king had stablished all the countries about London, then he let make Sir Kay seneschal of England; and Sir Baudwin of Britain was made constable; and Sir Ulfius was made chamberlain; and Sir Brastias was made warden to wait upon the north from Trent forwards, for it was that time the most part the king's enemies. But within few years after, Arthur won all the north, Scotland, and all that were under their obeissance. Also Wales, a part of it held against Arthur, but he overcame them all as he did the remnant through the noble prowess of himself and his knights of the Round Table.

HOW KING ARTHUR HELD IN WALES, AT A PENTECOST, A GREAT FEAST, AND WHAT KINGS AND LORDS CAME TO HIS FEAST. Then the king removed into Wales, and let cry a great feast that it should be holden at Pentecost after the incoronation of him at the city of Carlion. Unto the feast came king Lot of Lothian and of Orkney, with five hundred knights with him. Also there came to the feast King Uriens of Gore with four hundred knights with him. Also there came to that feast King Nentres of Garlot, with seven hundred knights with him. Also there came to the feast the king of Scotland with six hundred knights with him, and he was but a young man. Also there came to the feast a king that was called the king with the hundred knights, but he and his men were passing well bisene at all points. Also there came the king of Carados with five hundred knights. And King Arthur was glad of their coming, for he weened that all the kings and knights had come for great love, and to have done him worship at his feast, wherefore the king made great joy, and sent the kings and knights great presents. But the kings would none receive, but rebuked the messengers shamefully, and said they had no joy to receive no gifts of a beardless boy that was come of low blood, and sent him word they would none of his gifts, but that they were come to give him gifts with hard swords betwixt the neck and the shoulders: and therefore they came thither, so they told to the messengers plainly, for it was great shame to all them to see such a boy to have a rule of so noble a realm as this land was. With this answer the messengers departed and told to King Arthur this answer. Wherefore, by the advice of his barons, he took him to a strong tower with five hundred good

bisene = equipped.

men with him: and all the kings aforesaid in a manner laid a siege tofore him, but King Arthur was well victualed. And within fifteen days there came Merlin among them into the city of Carlion. Then all the kings were passing glad of Merlin, and asked him, For what cause is that boy Arthur made your king? Sirs, said Merlin, I shall tell you the cause, for he is King Uther Pendragon's son, born in wedlock, gotten on Igraine, the duke's wife of Tintagil. Then is he a bastard, they said all. Nay, said Merlin, after the death of the duke, more than three hours, was Arthur begotten, and thirteen days after King Uther wedded Igraine; and therefore I prove him he is no bastard, and who saith nay, he shall be king and overcome all his enemies; and, or he die, he shall be long king of all England, and have under his obeissance Wales, Ireland, and Scotland, and more realms than I will now rehearse. Some of the kings had marvel of Merlin's words, and deemed well that it should be as he said; and some of them laughed him to scorn, as King Lot; and more other called him a witch. But then were they accorded with Merlin, that King Arthur should come out and speak with the kings, and to come safe and to go safe, such assurance there was made. So Merlin went unto King Arthur, and told him how he had done, and bad him fear not, but come out boldly and speak with them, and spare them not, but answer them as their king and chieftain, for ye shall over-come them all whether they will or nill.

OF THE FIRST WAR THAT KING ARTHUR HAD, AND HOW HE WON THE FIELD. ❧Then King Arthur came out of his tower, and had under his gown a jesseraunte of double mail, and there went with him the Archbishop of Canterbury, and Sir Baudwin of Britain, and Sir Kay, and Sir Brastias: these were the men of most worship that were with him.

accorded = agreed.   jesseraunte = a cuirass.

And when they were met there was no meekness, but stout words on both sides; but always King Arthur answered them, and said he would make them to bow an he lived. Wherefore they departed with wrath, and King Arthur bad keep them well, and they bad the king keep him well. So the king returned him to the tower again and armed him and all his knights. What will ye do? said Merlin to the kings; ye were better for to stynte, for ye shall not here prevail though ye were ten times so many. Be we well advised to be afeard of a dream-reader? said King Lot. With that Merlin vanished away, and came to King Arthur, and bad him set on them fiercely; and in the meanwhile there were three hundred good men of the best that were with the kings, that went straight unto King Arthur, and that comforted him greatly. Sir, said Merlin to Arthur, fight not with the sword that ye had by miracle, till that ye see ye go unto the worse, then draw it out and do your best. So forthwithal King Arthur set upon them in their lodging. And Sir Baudwin, Sir Kay, and Sir Brastias slew on the right hand and on the left hand that it was marvel; and always King Arthur on horseback laid on with a sword, and did marvellous deeds of arms that many of the kings had great joy of his deeds and hardiness. Then King Lot brake out on the back side, and the king with the hundred knights, and King Carados, and set on Arthur fiercely behind him. With that Sir Arthur turned with his knights, and smote behind and before, and ever Sir Arthur was in the foremost press till his horse was slain underneath him. And therewith King Lot smote down King Arthur. With that his four knights received him and set him on horseback. Then he drew his sword Excalibur, but it was so bright in his enemies' eyes, that it gave light like thirty torches. And therewith he put them on back, and slew much people. And then the commons of Carlion arose with clubs and staves and slew many knights; but all the kings held them together with their knights that were left alive, and so fled and departed. And Merlin came unto Arthur, and counselled him to follow them no further.

 stynte = pause.

17

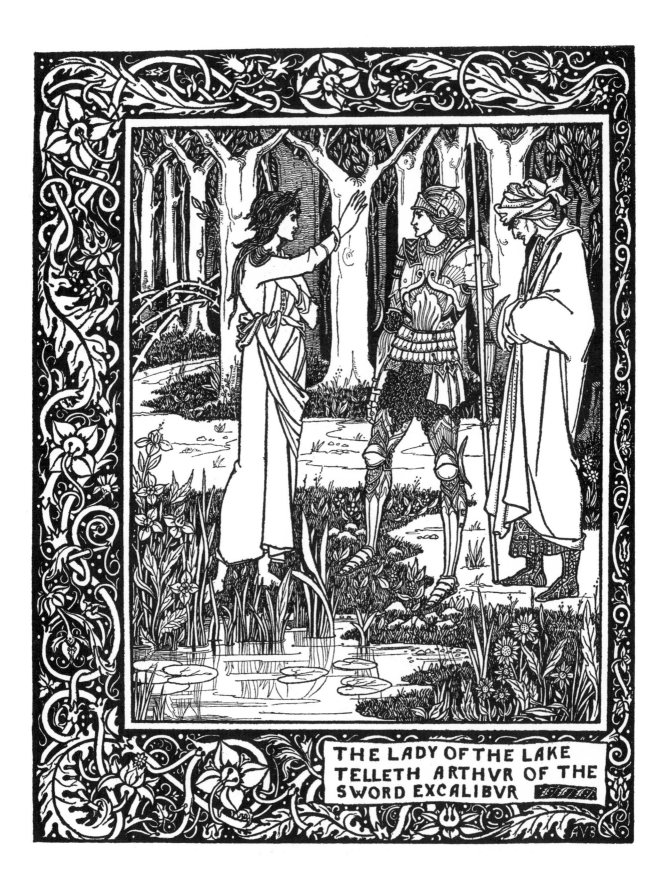

THE LADY OF THE LAKE
TELLETH ARTHVR OF THE
SWORD EXCALIBVR

Chapter xxiij.

Chapter xxiv.

Chap. xxv.

Chapter xxvj.

Chapter xxvij.

Explicit Liber Primus.

Book ij. Chapter j.

OF A DAMOSEL WHICH CAME GIRT WITH A SWORD FOR TO FIND A MAN OF SUCH VIRTUE TO DRAW IT OUT OF THE SCABBARD.

AFTER the death of Uther Pendragon reigned Arthur his son, the which had great war in his days for to get all England into his hand. For there were many kings within the realm of England, and in Wales, Scotland, and Cornwall. So it befell on a time when King Arthur was at London, there came a knight and told the king tidings how that the King Rience of North Wales had reared a great number of people, and were entered into the land, and burnt and slew the king's true liege people. If this be true, said Arthur, it were great shame unto mine estate but that he were mightily withstood. It is truth, said the knight, for I saw the host myself. Well, said the king, let make a cry, that all the lords, knights, and

23

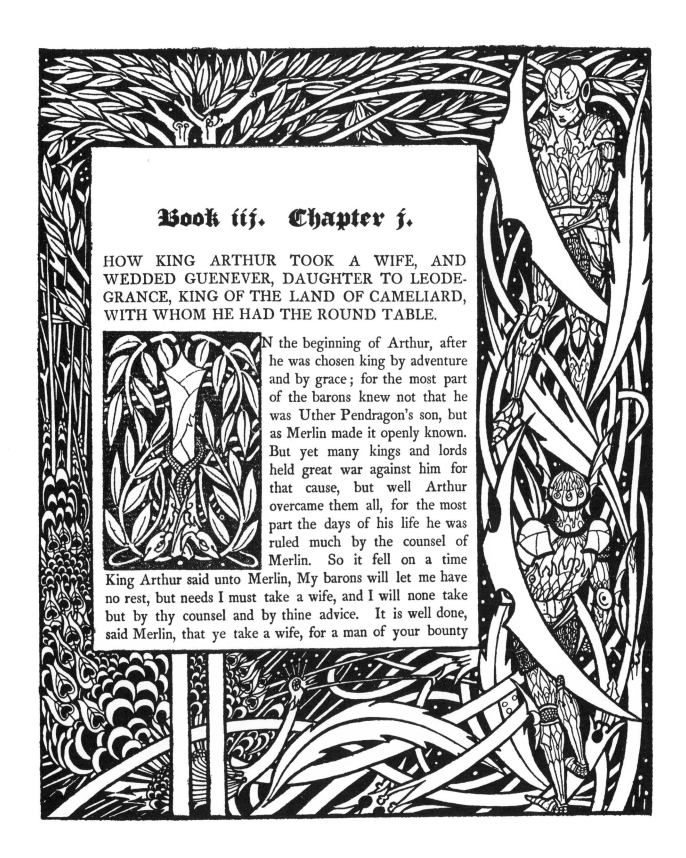

Book iij. Chapter j.

HOW KING ARTHUR TOOK A WIFE, AND
WEDDED GUENEVER, DAUGHTER TO LEODE-
GRANCE, KING OF THE LAND OF CAMELIARD,
WITH WHOM HE HAD THE ROUND TABLE.

N the beginning of Arthur, after
he was chosen king by adventure
and by grace; for the most part
of the barons knew not that he
was Uther Pendragon's son, but
as Merlin made it openly known.
But yet many kings and lords
held great war against him for
that cause, but well Arthur
overcame them all, for the most
part the days of his life he was
ruled much by the counsel of
Merlin. So it fell on a time
King Arthur said unto Merlin, My barons will let me have
no rest, but needs I must take a wife, and I will none take
but by thy counsel and by thine advice. It is well done,
said Merlin, that ye take a wife, for a man of your bounty

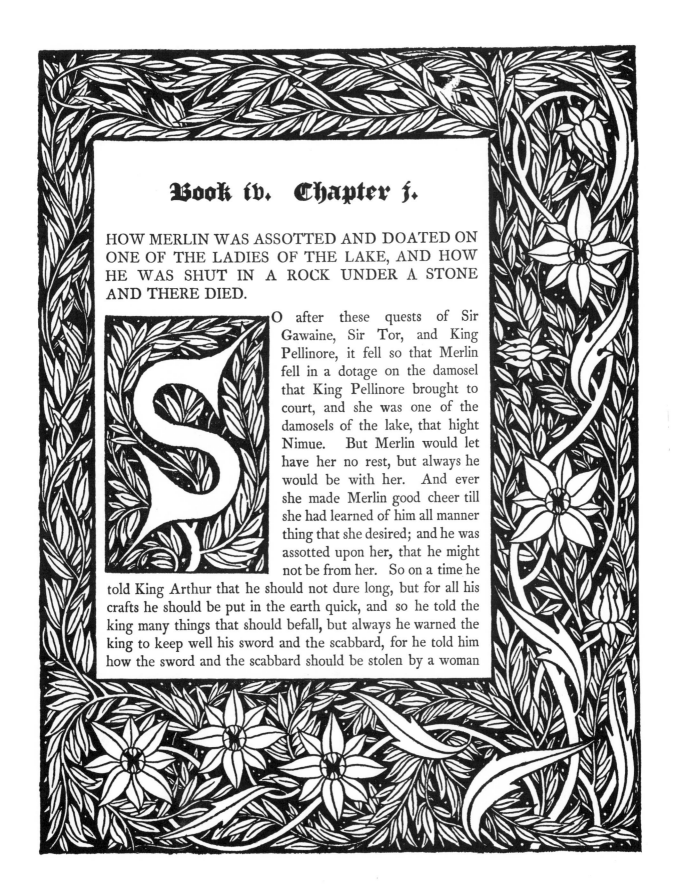

Book iv. Chapter j.

HOW MERLIN WAS ASSOTTED AND DOATED ON
ONE OF THE LADIES OF THE LAKE, AND HOW
HE WAS SHUT IN A ROCK UNDER A STONE
AND THERE DIED.

SO after these quests of Sir Gawaine, Sir Tor, and King Pellinore, it fell so that Merlin fell in a dotage on the damosel that King Pellinore brought to court, and she was one of the damosels of the lake, that hight Nimue. But Merlin would let have her no rest, but always he would be with her. And ever she made Merlin good cheer till she had learned of him all manner thing that she desired; and he was assotted upon her, that he might not be from her. So on a time he told King Arthur that he should not dure long, but for all his crafts he should be put in the earth quick, and so he told the king many things that should befall, but always he warned the king to keep well his sword and the scabbard, for he told him how the sword and the scabbard should be stolen by a woman

MERLIN AND
NIMVE

ARTHVR AND
THE STRANGE
MANTLE

Explicit Liber Quartus.
Incipit Liber Quintus.

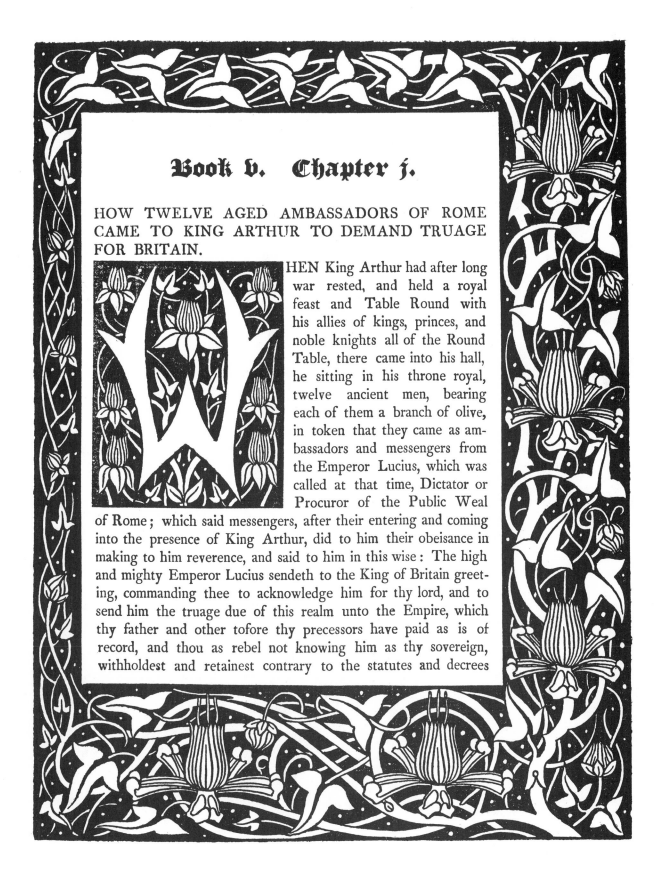

Book v. Chapter j.

HOW TWELVE AGED AMBASSADORS OF ROME
CAME TO KING ARTHUR TO DEMAND TRUAGE
FOR BRITAIN.

HEN King Arthur had after long war rested, and held a royal feast and Table Round with his allies of kings, princes, and noble knights all of the Round Table, there came into his hall, he sitting in his throne royal, twelve ancient men, bearing each of them a branch of olive, in token that they came as ambassadors and messengers from the Emperor Lucius, which was called at that time, Dictator or Procuror of the Public Weal of Rome; which said messengers, after their entering and coming into the presence of King Arthur, did to him their obeisance in making to him reverence, and said to him in this wise: The high and mighty Emperor Lucius sendeth to the King of Britain greeting, commanding thee to acknowledge him for thy lord, and to send him the truage due of this realm unto the Empire, which thy father and other tofore thy precessors have paid as is of record, and thou as rebel not knowing him as thy sovereign, withholdest and retainest contrary to the statutes and decrees

Book vj. Chapter j.

HOW SIR LAUNCELOT AND SIR LIONEL DEPARTED
FROM THE COURT, AND HOW SIR LIONEL LEFT
HIM SLEEPING AND WAS TAKEN.

SOON after that King Arthur was come from Rome into England, then all the knights of the Table Round resorted unto the king, and made many jousts and tournaments, and some there were that were but knights, which increased so in arms and worship that they passed all their fellows in prowess and noble deeds, and that was well proved on many; but in especial it was proved on Sir Launcelot du Lake, for in all tournaments and jousts and deeds of arms, both for life and death, he passed all other knights, and at no time he was never overcome but if it were by treason or enchantment, so Sir Launcelot increased so marvellously in worship, and in honour, therefore is he the first knight that the French book maketh mention of after King Arthur came from Rome. Wherefore Queen Guenever had him in great favour above all other knights, and in certain he loved the queen again above all

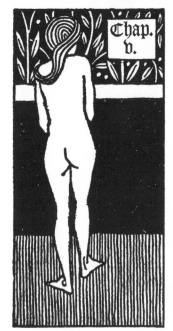

44

HOW. FOVR. QVEENS.
FOVND. LAVNCELOT.
SLEEPING.

SIR.LAVNCELOT.
AND.THE.WITCH.
HELLAWES. ✳✳✳

Book vij. Chapter j.

HOW BEAUMAINS CAME TO KING ARTHUR'S
COURT AND DEMANDED THREE PETITIONS OF
KING ARTHUR.

WHEN Arthur held his Round Table most plenour, it fortuned that he commanded that the high feast of Pentecost should be holden at a site and a castle, the which in those days was called Kynke Kenadonne upon the sands that marched nigh Wales. So ever the king had a custom that at the feast of Pentecost in especial, afore other feasts in the year, he would not go that day to meat until he had heard or seen of a great marvel. And for that custom all manner of strange adventures came before Arthur as at that feast before all other feasts. And so Sir Gawaine, a little tofore noon of the day of Pentecost, espied at a window three men upon horseback, and a dwarf on foot, and so the three men alit, and the dwarf kept their horses, and one of the three men was higher than the other twain by a foot and an half. Then Sir Gawaine went unto the king and said, Sir, go to your meat,

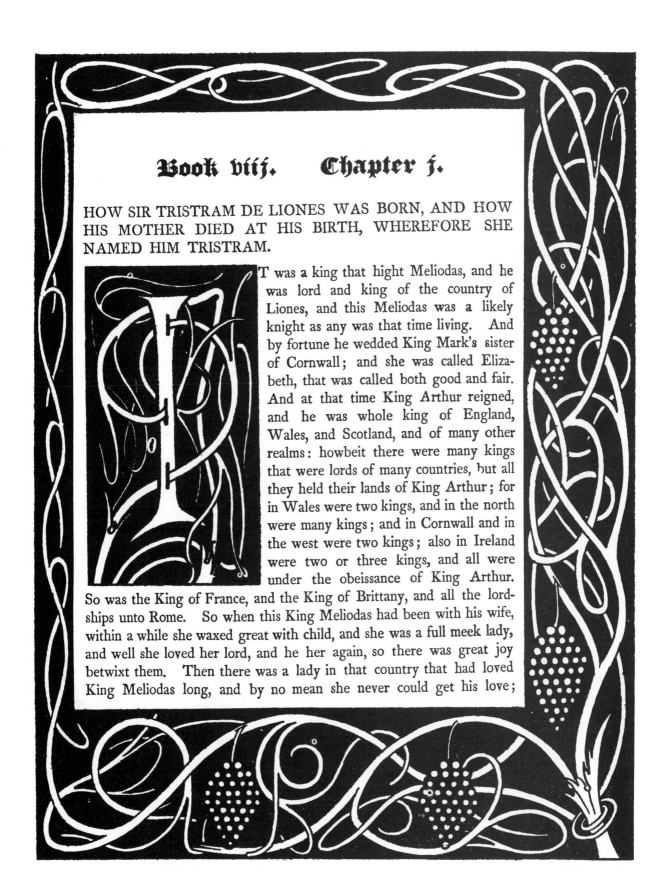

Book viij.   Chapter j.

HOW SIR TRISTRAM DE LIONES WAS BORN, AND HOW HIS MOTHER DIED AT HIS BIRTH, WHEREFORE SHE NAMED HIM TRISTRAM.

IT was a king that hight Meliodas, and he was lord and king of the country of Liones, and this Meliodas was a likely knight as any was that time living. And by fortune he wedded King Mark's sister of Cornwall; and she was called Elizabeth, that was called both good and fair. And at that time King Arthur reigned, and he was whole king of England, Wales, and Scotland, and of many other realms: howbeit there were many kings that were lords of many countries, but all they held their lands of King Arthur; for in Wales were two kings, and in the north were many kings; and in Cornwall and in the west were two kings; also in Ireland were two or three kings, and all were under the obeissance of King Arthur. So was the King of France, and the King of Brittany, and all the lordships unto Rome. So when this King Meliodas had been with his wife, within a while she waxed great with child, and she was a full meek lady, and well she loved her lord, and he her again, so there was great joy betwixt them. Then there was a lady in that country that had loved King Meliodas long, and by no mean she never could get his love;

HOW LA BEALE
ISOVD NVRSED
SIR TRISTRAM

63

HOW SIR TRISTRAM
DRANK OF THE
LOVE DRINK

Here leave we of Sir Lamorak and of
Sir Tristram. And here beginneth
the history of La Cote
Male Taile.

Morte Darthur

Second Portion
containing
Book viij to Book xj

The achieuing of the Sangreal

THE BIRTH LIFE AND ACTS OF KING ARTHUR OF HIS
NOBLE KNIGHTS OF THE ROUND TABLE THEIR
MARVELLOUS ENQUESTS AND ADVENTURES
THE ACHIEVING OF THE SAN GREAL
AND IN THE END LE MORTE DAR:
THUR WITH THE DOLOUROUS
DEATH AND DEPARTING
OUT OF THIS WORLD
OF THEM ALL.

THE TEXT AS WRIT:
TEN BY SIR THOMAS MALORY
AND IMPRINTED BY WILLIAM CAXTON
AT WESTMINSTER THE YEAR MCCCCLXXXV AND
NOW SPELLED IN MODERN STYLE. WITH AN INTRO:
DUCTION BY PROFESSOR RHYS AND EMBELLISHED WITH
MANY ORIGINAL DESIGNS BY AUBREY BEARDSLEY. MDCCCXCIV.

Title page for Volumes II and III

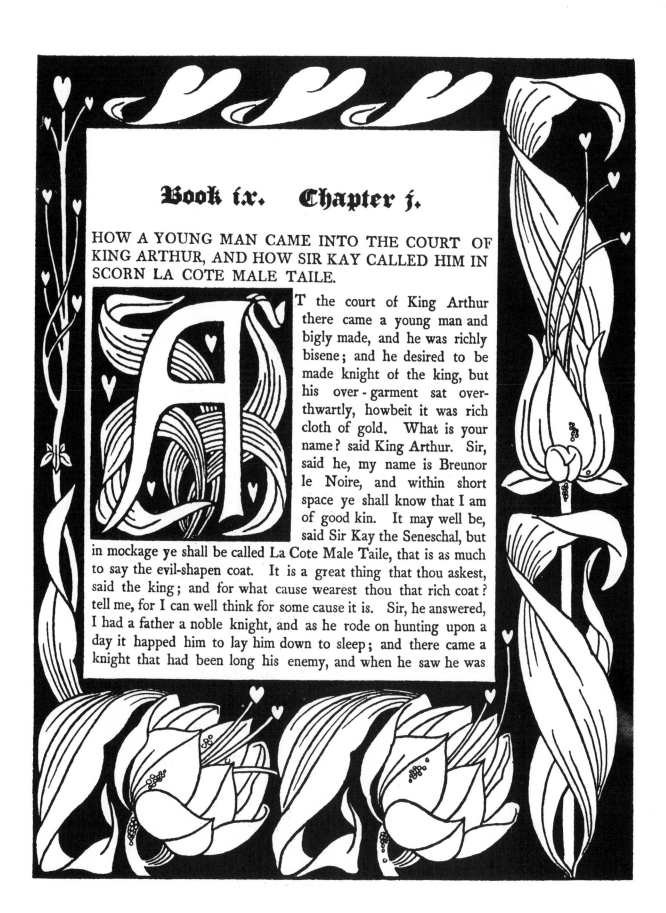

Book ix.   Chapter j.

HOW A YOUNG MAN CAME INTO THE COURT OF
KING ARTHUR, AND HOW SIR KAY CALLED HIM IN
SCORN LA COTE MALE TAILE.

AT the court of King Arthur there came a young man and bigly made, and he was richly bisene; and he desired to be made knight of the king, but his over-garment sat overthwartly, howbeit it was rich cloth of gold. What is your name? said King Arthur. Sir, said he, my name is Breunor le Noire, and within short space ye shall know that I am of good kin. It may well be, said Sir Kay the Seneschal, but in mockage ye shall be called La Cote Male Taile, that is as much to say the evil-shapen coat. It is a great thing that thou askest, said the king; and for what cause wearest thou that rich coat? tell me, for I can well think for some cause it is. Sir, he answered, I had a father a noble knight, and as he rode on hunting upon a day it happed him to lay him down to sleep; and there came a knight that had been long his enemy, and when he saw he was

HOW LA BEALE
ISOVD WROTE TO
SIR TRISTRAM

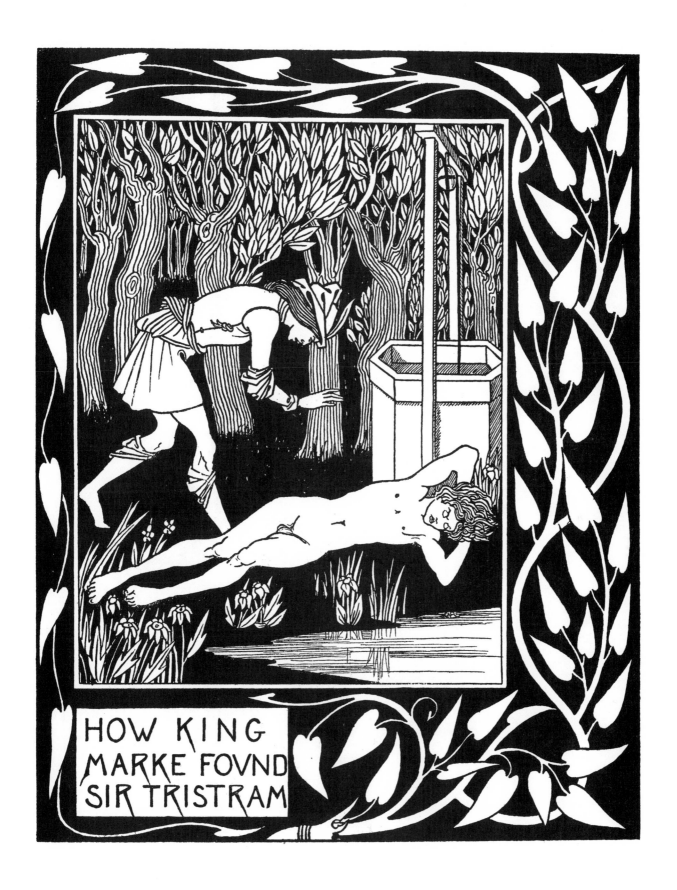

HOW KING
MARKE FOVND
SIR TRISTRAM

HOW. MORGAN. LE
FAY. GAVE. A. SHIELD.
TO. SIR. TRISTRAM

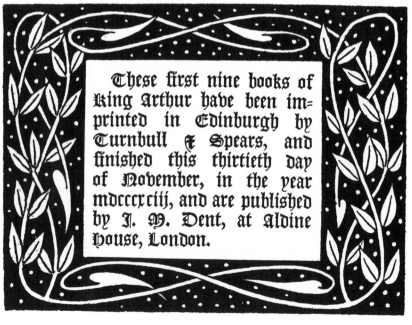

These first nine books of King Arthur have been imprinted in Edinburgh by Turnbull & Spears, and finished this thirtieth day of November, in the year mdcccxciii, and are published by J. M. Dent, at Aldine House, London.

Book x. Chapter j.

HOW SIR TRISTRAM JOUSTED, AND SMOTE DOWN KING ARTHUR, BECAUSE HE TOLD HIM NOT THE CAUSE WHY HE BARE THAT SHIELD.

AND if so be ye can descrive what ye bear, ye are worthy to bear the arms. As for that, said Sir Tristram, I will answer you, this shield was given me, not desired, of Queen Morgan le Fay; and as for me, I can not descrive these arms, for it is no point of my charge, and yet I trust to God to bear them with worship. Truly, said King Arthur, ye ought not to bear none arms but if ye wist what ye bear: but I pray you tell me your name. To what intent, said Sir Tristram? For I would wit, said Arthur. Sir, ye shall not wit as at this time. Then shall ye and I do battle together, said King Arthur. Why, said Sir Tristram, will ye do battle with me but if I tell you my name? and that little needeth you an ye were a man of worship, for ye have seen me this day have had great travail, and therefore ye

Chap.
xv.

Chap.
xvi.

Chap.
xviii.

Chap.
xvii.

Chap.
xix.

How King Mark and Sir Dinadan heard Sir
Palomides making great sorrow and mourn-
ing for La Beale Isoud.

La Beale Isoud at Joyous Gard.

102

108

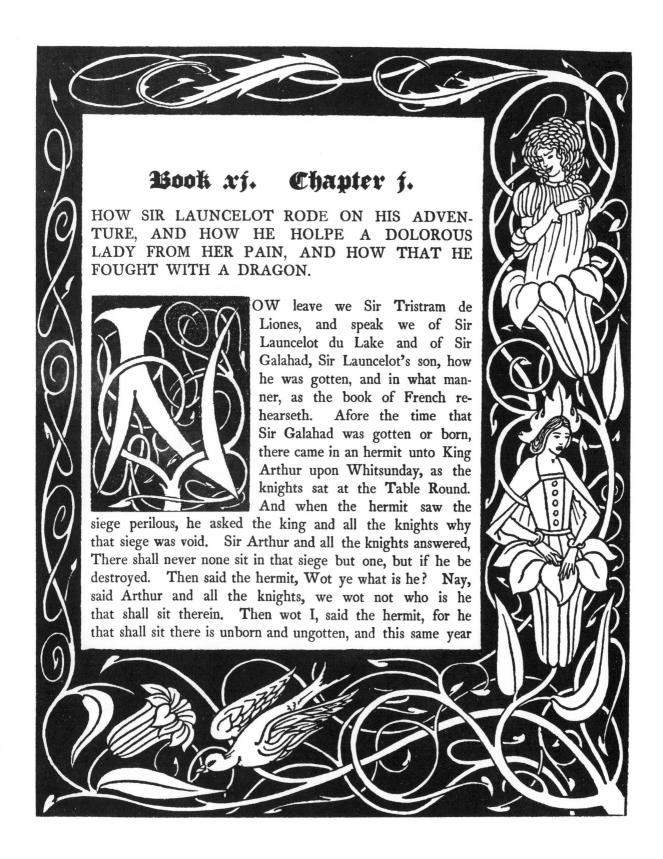

Book xj.   Chapter j.

HOW SIR LAUNCELOT RODE ON HIS ADVEN-
TURE, AND HOW HE HOLPE A DOLOROUS
LADY FROM HER PAIN, AND HOW THAT HE
FOUGHT WITH A DRAGON.

NOW leave we Sir Tristram de Liones, and speak we of Sir Launcelot du Lake and of Sir Galahad, Sir Launcelot's son, how he was gotten, and in what manner, as the book of French rehearseth. Afore the time that Sir Galahad was gotten or born, there came in an hermit unto King Arthur upon Whitsunday, as the knights sat at the Table Round. And when the hermit saw the siege perilous, he asked the king and all the knights why that siege was void. Sir Arthur and all the knights answered, There shall never none sit in that siege but one, but if he be destroyed. Then said the hermit, Wot ye what is he? Nay, said Arthur and all the knights, we wot not who is he that shall sit therein. Then wot I, said the hermit, for he that shall sit there is unborn and ungotten, and this same year

111

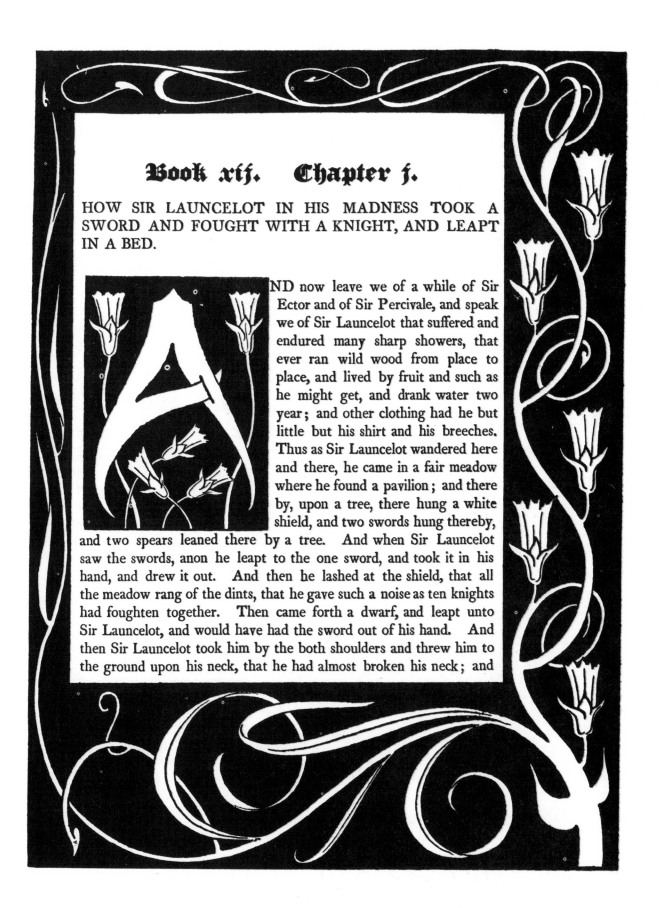

Book xij.   Chapter j.

HOW SIR LAUNCELOT IN HIS MADNESS TOOK A
SWORD AND FOUGHT WITH A KNIGHT, AND LEAPT
IN A BED.

ND now leave we of a while of Sir
Ector and of Sir Percivale, and speak
we of Sir Launcelot that suffered and
endured many sharp showers, that
ever ran wild wood from place to
place, and lived by fruit and such as
he might get, and drank water two
year; and other clothing had he but
little but his shirt and his breeches.
Thus as Sir Launcelot wandered here
and there, he came in a fair meadow
where he found a pavilion; and there
by, upon a tree, there hung a white
shield, and two swords hung thereby,
and two spears leaned there by a tree.   And when Sir Launcelot
saw the swords, anon he leapt to the one sword, and took it in his
hand, and drew it out.   And then he lashed at the shield, that all
the meadow rang of the dints, that he gave such a noise as ten knights
had foughten together.   Then came forth a dwarf, and leapt unto
Sir Launcelot, and would have had the sword out of his hand.   And
then Sir Launcelot took him by the both shoulders and threw him to
the ground upon his neck, that he had almost broken his neck; and

How Sir Launcelot was known by
Dame Elaine.

117

Book xiij. Chapter j.

HOW AT THE VIGIL OF THE FEAST OF PENTECOST
ENTERED INTO THE HALL BEFORE KING ARTHUR
A DAMOSEL, AND DESIRED SIR LAUNCELOT FOR
TO COME AND DUB A KNIGHT, AND HOW HE
WENT WITH HER.

AT the vigil of Pentecost, when all the fellowship of the Round Table were come unto Camelot, and there heard their service, and the tables were set ready to the meat, right so entered into the hall a full fair gentlewoman on horseback, that had ridden full fast, for her horse was all besweated. Then she there alit, and came before the king and saluted him; and he said, Damosel, God thee bless. Sir, said she, for God's sake say me where Sir Launcelot is. Yonder ye may see him, said the king. Then she went unto Launcelot and said, Sir Launcelot, I salute you on King Pelles' behalf, and I require you come on with me hereby into a forest. Then Sir Launcelot asked her with whom she dwelled. I dwell, said she, with King Pelles. What will ye with me? said Launcelot. Ye shall know, said she, when ye come thither. Well, said he, I will

Book xiv. Chapter j.

HOW SIR PERCIVALE CAME TO A RECLUSE AND ASKED COUNSEL, AND HOW SHE TOLD HIM THAT SHE WAS HIS AUNT.

NOW saith the tale, that when Sir Launcelot was ridden after Sir Galahad, the which had all these adventures above said, Sir Percivale turned again unto the recluse, where he deemed to have tidings of that knight that Launcelot followed. And so he kneeled at her window, and the recluse opened it and asked Sir Percivale what he would. Madam, he said, I am a knight of King Arthur's court, and my name is Sir Percivale de Galis. When the recluse heard his name she had great joy of him, for mickle she had loved him tofore any other knight, for she ought to do so, for she was his aunt. And then she commanded the gates to be opened, and there he had all the cheer that she might make him, and all that

Book xv. Chapter j.

HOW SIR LAUNCELOT CAME TO A CHAPEL, WHERE HE FOUND DEAD, IN A WHITE SHIRT, A MAN OF RELIGION, OF AN HUNDRED WINTER OLD.

HEN the hermit had kept Sir Launcelot three days, the hermit gat him an horse, an helm, and a sword. And then he departed about the hour of noon. And then he saw a little house. And when he came near he saw a chapel, and there beside he saw an old man that was clothed all in white full richly; and then Sir Launcelot said, God save you. God keep you, said the good man, and make you a good knight. Then Sir Launcelot alit and entered into the chapel, and there he saw an old man dead, in a white shirt of passing fine cloth. Sir, said the good man, this man that is dead ought not to be in such clothing as ye see him in, for in that he brake the oath of his order, for he hath been more

Book xvj.   Chapter j.

HOW SIR GAWAINE WAS NIGH WEARY OF THE QUEST OF THE SANGREAL, AND OF HIS MARVELLOUS DREAM.

HEN Sir Gawaine was departed from his fellowship he rode long without any adventure. For he found not the tenth part of adventure as he was wont to do. For Sir Gawaine rode from Whitsuntide until Michaelmas and found none adventure that pleased him. So on a day it befel Gawaine met with Sir Ector de Maris, and either made great joy of other that it were marvel to tell. And so they told every each other, and complained them greatly that they could find none adventure. Truly, said Sir Gawaine unto Sir Ector, I am nigh weary of this quest, and loth I am to follow further in strange countries. One thing marvelled me, said Sir Ector, I have met with twenty knights, fellows of mine, and all they complain as I do. I have marvel, said Sir Gawaine, where that Sir Launcelot your brother is. Truly, said Sir Ector,

How a devil in Woman's likeness would have tempted Sir Bors

Book xvij. Chapter j.

HOW SIR GALAHAD FOUGHT AT A TOURNA-
MENT, AND HOW HE WAS KNOWN OF SIR
GAWAINE AND SIR ECTOR DE MARIS.

OW saith this story, when Galahad had rescued Percivale from the twenty knights he yede then into a waste forest wherein he rode many journeys; and he found many adventures the which he brought to an end, whereof the story maketh here no mention. Then he took his way to the sea on a day and it befel as he passed by a castle where was a wonder tournament, but they without had done so much that they within were put to the worse, yet were they within good knights enough. When Galahad saw that those within were at so great a mischief that men slew them at the entry of the castle, then he thought to help them, and put a spear forth and smote the first that he fell to the earth, and the spear brake to pieces. Then he

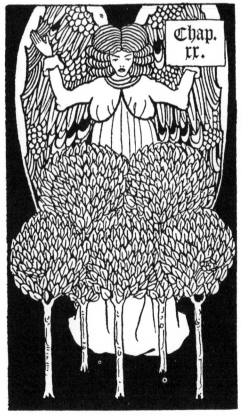

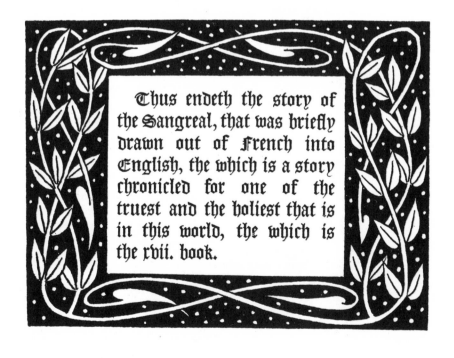

Thus endeth the story of the Sangreal, that was briefly drawn out of French into English, the which is a story chronicled for one of the truest and the holiest that is in this world, the which is the xvii. book.

Book xviij.   Chapter j.

OF THE JOY OF KING ARTHUR AND THE
QUEEN HAD OF THE ACHIEVEMENT OF THE
SANGREAL; AND HOW LAUNCELOT FELL TO
HIS OLD LOVE AGAIN.

SO after the quest of the Sangreal was fulfilled, and all knights that were left on live were come again unto the Table Round, as the book of the Sangreal maketh mention, then was there great joy in the court; and in especial King Arthur and Queen Guenever made great joy of the remnant that were come home, and passing glad was the king and the queen of Sir Launcelot and of Sir Bors, for they had been passing long away in the quest of the Sangreal. Then, as the book saith, Sir Launcelot began to resort unto Queen Guenever again, and forgat the promise and the perfection that he made in the quest. For, as the book saith, had not Sir Launcelot been in his privy thoughts and in his mind so set inwardly

Chap.
r.

Chap.
rj.

Chapter
viij.

Chap.
rij.

Chap.
riv.

Chapter
riij.

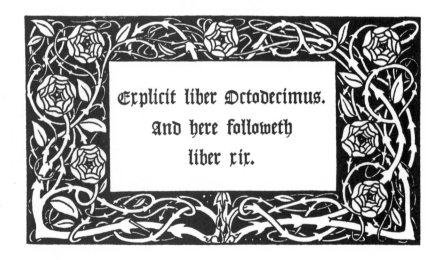

Explicit liber Octodecimus.
And here followeth
liber rir.

Book xix. Chapter j.

HOW QUEEN GUENEVER RODE ON MAYING
WITH CERTAIN KNIGHTS OF THE ROUND
TABLE AND CLAD ALL IN GREEN.

O it befell in the month of May, Queen Guenever called unto her, knights of the Table Round; and she gave them warning that early upon the morrow she would ride on Maying into woods and fields beside Westminster. And I warn you that there be none of you but that he be well horsed, and that ye all be clothed in green, either in silk outher in cloth; and I shall bring with me ten ladies, and every knight shall have a lady behind him, and every knight shall have a squire and two yeomen; and I will that ye all be well horsed. So they made them ready in the freshest manner. And these were the names of the knights: Sir Kay le Seneschal, Sir Agravaine, Sir Brandiles, Sir Sagramore le

How Queen Guenever rode on Maying.

148

Book xx. Chapter j.

HOW SIR AGRAVAINE AND SIR MORDRED WERE BUSY UPON SIR GAWAINE FOR TO DISCLOSE THE LOVE BETWEEN SIR LAUNCELOT AND QUEEN GUENEVER.

IN May when every lusty heart flourisheth and bourgeoneth, for as the season is lusty to behold and comfortable, so man and woman rejoice and gladden of summer coming with his fresh flowers: for winter with his rough winds and blasts causeth a lusty man and woman to cower, and sit fast by the fire. So in this season, as in the month of May, it befell a great anger and unhap that stinted not till the flower of chivalry of all the world was destroyed and slain; and all was long upon two unhappy knights, the which were named Agravaine and Sir Mordred, that were brethren unto Sir Gawaine. For this Sir Agravaine and Sir Mordred had ever a privy hate unto the queen Dame Guenever and to Sir Launcelot, and daily and nightly they ever watched upon Sir Launcelot.

155

Book xxj. Chapter j.

HOW SIR MORDRED PRESUMED AND TOOK ON HIM TO BE KING OF ENGLAND, AND WOULD HAVE MARRIED THE QUEEN, HIS UNCLE'S WIFE.

AS Sir Mordred was ruler of all England, he did do make letters as though that they came from beyond the sea, and the letters specified that King Arthur was slain in battle with Sir Launcelot. Wherefore Sir Mordred made a parliament, and called the lords together, and there he made them to choose him king; and so was he crowned at Canterbury, and held a feast there fifteen days; and afterward he drew him unto Winchester, and there he took the Queen Guenever, and said plainly that he would wed her which was his uncle's wife, and his father's wife. And so he made ready for the feast, and a day prefixed that they should be wedded; wherefore Queen Guenever was passing heavy. But she durst

163

164

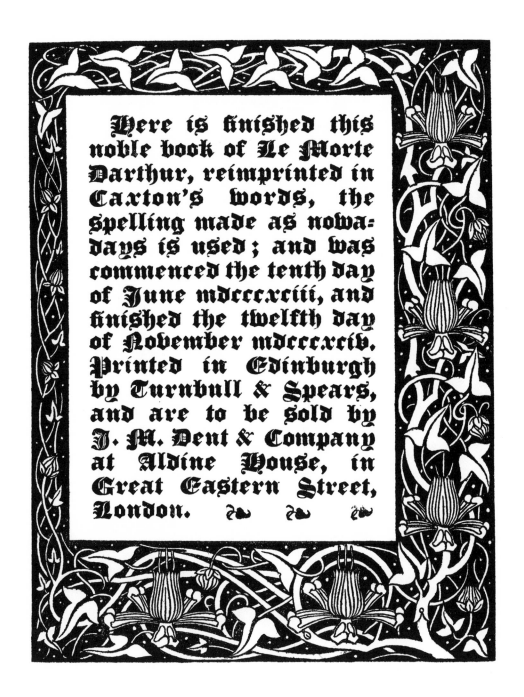

Here is finished this noble book of Le Morte Darthur, reimprinted in Caxton's words, the spelling made as nowadays is used; and was commenced the tenth day of June mdcccxciii, and finished the twelfth day of November mdcccxciv. Printed in Edinburgh by Turnbull & Spears, and are to be sold by J. M. Dent & Company at Aldine House, in Great Eastern Street, London.

FOOTNOTE ORNAMENTS

(These footnote ornaments are repeated in various combinations throughout the book.)

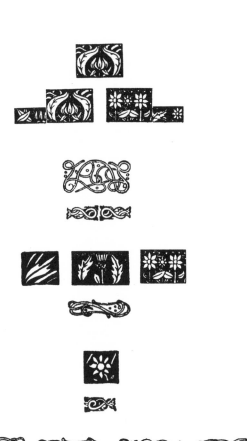

Binding design for "Le Morte Darthur"

171